# The World of Hypnosis

By: Gabriel Holmes

# CONTENTS

Acknowledgments

1   Intro to Hypnosis                    Pg # 7

2   World of Hypnosis                    Pg # 21

3   Hypnosis and the Media               Pg # 28

4   Hypnotized Easily                    Pg # 32

5   The Motivational                     Pg # 35

6   Sleep and Relax                      Pg # 42

7   The Conclusion                       Pg # 51

Acknowledgements:

Thanks you to John Sievers and Sali Holmes for their excellent skills in editing!

Thank you to Eli Holmes for adding his knowledge of psychological aspects to the writing.

# Chapter 1
# INTRO TO HYPNOSIS

Hypnosis surrounds you. Throughout the day, the week and your life, whether you realize it or not, you are being hypnotized. Hypnosis, put into simple terms, is the power of suggestion and it happens to you every day. Frequently, hypnotism results from interactions with the media. This raises the question, "Who is attempting to influence me and why?"

This book will illustrate the principles of hypnosis and how they are being used in today's world. Sales is one of the most frequent applications of hypnosis. Automobiles, perfumes, sporting goods, and the latest movies are all sold using hypnosis. This book will explain some of the hypnotic techniques used by the advertising industry.

The power of the mind is truly formidable. What makes one have the ability to remain calm while on a rollercoaster while another person can be in a state of shock? What are the questions and suggestions that we ask ourselves prior to and during these events that continue to create the events? Can someone become calm instantly? Can a stage hypnotist take a total stranger and have them in a sleep-like state in 3 minutes? The answer is YES!! The use of hypnosis is all around us, and much can be learned from studying hypnosis and its practice.

In an age where screens surround us, we are constantly encountering screen induced hypnosis. For instance, we frequently allow movies to entrance us. If you go to a theatre and sit down to watch a scary movie, you may experience a real feeling of terror. During this event, your heart will race, and your body will tense up as if you are actually one of the characters within the movie. You could actually experience fear while sitting in the theatre, yet there may be as many as 200 people sitting around you, and you are perfectly safe. Your mind has created the sensation of fear by interpreting the images and ideas presented on screen, yet you are in no danger.

How many people looked at a shower curtain completely differently after watching Psycho? Fear is a created through the power of the mind, and being on the rollercoaster is completely safe by most standards. Despite this safety, many roller coaster passengers become manic and sweat, allow their heart rates to increase, and feel terror. If you are a person that dislikes roller coasters, and you simply just imagine yourself on a roller coaster, you may also experience these same effects. On stage during a hypnosis show, a hypnotist can create the same roller coaster experience through the use of mental imagery, and the subject will feel genuine fear. The words we tell ourselves or the words that the hypnotist utilizes can influence or "hypnotize" us to believe these unrealistic situations.

Hypnosis can be used in many different ways besides on the stage. Hypnosis can be used with sleep, selling a suggestion, increasing performance in sports, and numerous other applications that will be explored within this book.

## Been Hypnotized

Have you ever been hypnotized? Many times I will stand up in front of a theatre and ask an audience of four or five hundred people, "Who has ever been hypnotized by a hypnotist before?" Often I will have only six or seven people actually raise their hands. Everyone within the room has been hypnotized to varying degrees, but very few have been directly hypnotized by a hypnotist before. Everyone has been hypnotized at some level, but they are just not aware of it. The following examples demonstrates the hypnotic states that people enter throughout their daily lives.

a) Have you ever driven past your house when your intention was to go home? Driving is one of the most hypnotic things that we can do. We can go on a long road trip and suddenly hours go by without remembering the route that we took. We can pass numerous towns, lakes and pastures while not remembering a good deal of the route. Driving creates the sleep-like hypnotic state where you are focused on the painted white lines twenty or thirty feet in front of you. We often react subconsciously to situations on the road without consciously thinking about the tasks of driving at hand. When we first learn to drive as a teenager, we are creating a much more conscious state with both hands on the wheel and attempting to notice everything around us. After years of driving, we create a more nap-like state while on the road. This state might be called a subconscious state. Some incredibly hypnotic situations can arise for anyone who has driven through snow, especially on a dark evening. The snowflakes falling with the white lines going by create a very repetitious and hypnotic state for the driver. It is a similar effect to the use of a flashing light that hypnotists will often use in order to help hypnotize someone.

b) Have you ever gone out and bought something and later had no clue why you bought it? Television is one of the most hypnotic mediums within the world today. We often lounge into our favorite chair or couch as we stare at the television screen, while the flickers of the screen create a deep hypnotic state. During the breaks within the show, commercials are then fed to us while we are in this hypnotic state. Days or weeks later while out shopping we say to ourselves, "I need to have that item." That item was the same one we saw on TV while in a hypnotic state. The advertising industry frequently uses hypnosis to sell products.

c) Have you ever been married? Has that husband or wife ever gotten you to do something you did not want to do? We all have used the power of suggestion to our benefit at times. Yes, sometimes you are doing the cost benefit analysis, but sometimes you get used to simply obeying, and doing it without thinking consciously about the suggestion. A parent can have a similar effect on a child by the child simply obeying the command. At times we have all stopped ourselves, and consciously ask ourselves, "Why am I doing this?" We are often just blankly following the suggestion or hypnotic command of the person we know.

d) Have you ever become very absorbed in a movie and then it is suddenly over? After the movie, you are left wondering where the time has gone? Movies can slip us into a hypnotic state by seeing the flickering screen in a dark room with a fixed point. When we go to a theatre or sit at home and watch a scary movie, we can use our powerful imagination to visualize a killer coming around the corner within the movie. We feel AS IF we are there and we feel as if we are a character within the movie. While watching the movie, our heart could beat faster and we may feel anxiety from the movie. We are acting in our imagination AS IF we are present within the scene yet we are sitting within the theater. One can be scared within the movie theater yet there are 300 other people sitting around us watching the movie. The movie has hypnotized our mind into believing the scenes are truly real. Many people go to movies to escape and feel as if we are somewhere as an action adventurer like Indiana Jones or a spy like James Bond. We can feel as if we are experiencing a love story or thriller and become completely involved within the movie. Then when the movie is over, sometimes we get so entrenched with the movie or hypnotized that we have to remind ourselves that we were only watching a movie. . Sometimes you can be in a movie and have to go to the bathroom. We then walk out of the movie and then have to remind ourselves that we are just in a movie. This can be very similar to waking up from a dream and having to pinch ourselves and remind ourselves that we were just sleeping.

Movies are truly one of the most hypnotic scenarios we can place ourselves in with the world today.

Hypnosis is the power of suggestion. We have all been unknowingly influenced on a daily basis, but being aware of the outward hypnotic influences can help us throughout the day. An awareness of hypnotic influences can increase our self control. Understanding hypnosis and its uses can help us in numerous areas of our lives.

## What is Hypnosis?

Hypnosis comes from the Greek word Hypnos, which means sleep. There are as many definitions of hypnosis as there are hypnotists practicing within the field. More than anything, hypnosis is an altered state where the person who is hypnotized is in an extremely focused state. Everyone has been completely focused on a book or movie and has had no real consciousness of the activities going on around them at the time. This focused state is a type of hypnosis and we experience it frequently throughout our days. During this state of focused attention, we are not aware of the fan making noise above our head or of the birds flying by outside. We are simply hyper focused on the interesting book or movie that we are taking in. We are in a focused hypnotic state.

When reading this book keep in mind it is not intended to completely cover all the research and academic aspects of hypnosis but instead to educate people how hypnosis and its variants affect our everyday lives. John F. Kihlstrom Ph.D., who has researched hypnosis for decades, eloquently states hypnosis to be "an altered state of consciousness that occurs within a particular interpersonal setting." Altered states of consciousness are frequent in our experiences. For example, many people drink alcohol. Think of how many times when "buzzed" or drunk, those drinking have been subject to suggestions from others. Many people take medications that alter their consciousness such as painkillers, psychotropics, and others. Food also changes our state of consciousness. Most of us have eaten today, and food is a chemical that alters our state, mood and energy. Coffee or caffeinated beverages, "pick us up." The critical thinker may say, yes, but those are drugs or chemicals. The point is, we have many different altered states of consciousness and to varying degrees, depending on each, we are open to suggestion. Yes, some altered states are self-induced with chemicals or emotional states. The unavoidable point is that we alter our state co sistantly, so hypnosis is simply another altered state of consciousness in which we are particularly open to suggestion.

Another important aspect of hypnotism is the element of its interpersonal setting. When people think of hypnosis they may have seen "stage shows". I have performed more than 1,300 shows to date. These stage shows are a particular setting where I ask for volunteers to come up on stage to be hypnotized. Here, there is a very clearly defined agreement that an audience member will be brought up on stage, and hypnotized. These are the stereotypical situations that immediately come to mind when the general public thinks of hypnosis. However, one of the points of this book is to suggest that many other groups manipulate and utilize the concepts of hypnosis to their advantage. Having this conceptualization of hypnosis in mind, realize that there
are daily altered states that of consciousness that occur without our awareness.

## The Relaxing Place

It is easiest to get into the state of being hypnotized in a relaxing setting. The ultimate set-up for a stage hypnotist to hypnotize a group of subjects or volunteers is a dark and relaxed area such as a theatre. Stage hypnotists want to have the chairs set back far enough from the audience on stage to avoid distractions from the crowd. The hypnotist may then play soothing background music in order to drown out any excess noise such as coughing, squeaking chairs or other distractions from the audience. Within a theatre, the noise that can be generated from the audience can be significant. On stage, conversation can easily be heard from the front rows of people in a theatre. (A true benefit of being a stage hypnotist is the ability to perform shows in many beautiful and different theatres around the country and world.) The theatre, creates a relaxing place on stage which is an ideal place for a hypnosis show.

A clinical hypnotist prefers to have a relaxed couch in a dimly lit room for the client or hypnotic subject, or to relax in a deep chair. Hypnotherapists prefer to have a relaxing chair for the client with ambient music playing in the background. Relaxing music is sometimes also played behind the subject while the hypnotist starts the person into a deep relaxed hypnotic state.

The worst place to hypnotize someone would be in a public place like a busy café with distractions and noise all around. The fewer distractions, the easier the person will slip into a hypnotic state. Hypnotists look for the hypnotized subject to get into the focused state and then stay within that state during the show or the hypnotherapy session. The better the surrounding for the hypnotic state, the more deeply hypnotised the subjects will be. The deeper the person goes in a state of hypnosis, the more powerful and effective the suggestions will be for the client or stage performer. Thus the premier need for a good session or show is a relaxing place to attain the deepest hypnotic state.

## Hypnosis Show

Not everyone has seen a hypnosis show, and, for the sake of understanding hypnosis better, it is important to understand what a typical show is like. A hypnosis show usually takes place in a theatre where the audience files in and fills the seats. The hypnotist is introduced and does a short introduction describing hypnosis, which will later be followed by some full audience participation demonstrating the use of hypnosis.

The hypnotist will first identify a group of suggestible subjects to use during the show based on audience participation that includes the use of suggestibility tests. The most suggestible subjects come up on stage, and usually 15 to 20 participants will be selected. Next, the hypnotist guides the group using a hypnotic induction. This induction uses relaxation techniques that guide the subjects into a state of hypnosis. This usually takes eight to twelve minutes depending on the group and the hypnotist's skill. Once the participants are under a state of hypnosis, the hypnotist gives suggestions and the subjects will then respond to the suggestions. The hypnotist gives numerous unusual suggestions to create an entertaining spectacle. The suggestions at the beginning of the show could be to act as if you are driving a car. The subjects will then grasp the non-existent steering wheel and pretend they are really driving. The next suggestion could be to imitate canoeing on a beautiful lake, approaching an island, grabbing binoculars and zooming into the island. The participants will grab their binoculars and adjust them as if they are really looking at the island. Next, the hypnotist will say, " Now, you see some people on the island and you notice that they are listening to the most hilarious story you have ever heard. On the count of three, you will laugh harder than you have ever laughed before." On three, the participants will burst out into all consuming laughter.

Some of the suggestions that could be later in the show might be to have the participants act as if they are Steve Irwin the crocodile hunter scoping out new animals in the forest. The hypnotized person on stage will assume the Australian accent and act as if he or she is excited about the reaction of the animals. One of the participants might say, " Crikey, look at that alligator. Look at the jaws on that alligator. A beauty isn't it?"

Another suggestion could be to imitate a singer on a talent show. The participants will sing with great glee a song they may only vaguely know. One person could sing as if they are Justin Bieber and shout out the lyrics to one of his big tunes. Another person on stage may be influenced to act as if he or she is Simon Cowell critiquing the singers in a sarcastic way with a British accent.

Another example of the hyper suggestibility during a stage show is to have the participant forget his or her name. The hypnotist will then ask the participant's name, and the participant will try with all their might to remember. The subject will act very perplexed, but he or she will be unable to remember. Influencing someone to forget his or her name is a feat that amazes audiences. The hypnotist can then say, " You will remember your name and you will act excited as if you are a little kid." The participants will then practically jump up and down with child-like excitement finally knowing his or her name.

Many participants are hypnotized deeply enough they will act out suggestions in a completely uninhibited manner without worrying about the audience or their peers' perception. Hypnosis has this ability to break down the fear one would have to perform and creates great performers that act out the hypnotist's commands with complete confidence. The hypnosis show turns into a sort of comedic improvisational session between the hypnotist and the hypnotized subjects continuing these creative acts or skits.

After about 50 minutes or so of these improvisational hypnotic demonstrations, the hypnotist will wake the subjects from their state of hypnosis. The hypnotist will go down the line of people and ask, "How long do you think you have been on stage?" Most of the subjects will respond, "I just got up here."

The majority of the subjects will be amazed that they were under a state of hypnosis performing for the audience for almost an hour. To them it might have only felt like a couple of minutes. The subjects will then return to the audience, and the hypnotist will give a brief closing discussion about hypnosis and how it can be used in their daily lives. The audience will clap and the show will be finished. The participants' friends will show them or describe their hypnotized antics. The people will then gradually file out of the auditorium, and the theatre is quiet again as the show is now completely over.

## The YES/NO Factor

Hypnosis bypasses your critical thinking. Another way of thinking of this is that hypnosis temporarily takes away the yes/no factor. This is the area of conscious decision that takes place where one decides whether or not to act. Hypnosis takes away the fear to participate in an event. The success of a good stage show depends on the subjects on stage performing with great confidence to create humorous situations. Normally, they never take such chances. When the subjects on stage are given a command, they just DO the command without thinking of it or the potentially embarrassing consequences of their performance. The subjects sing, dance and perform in front of 500 to 600 people when normally they would never even get up in front of the audience let alone perform in front of them. The true success of a hypnosis show depends on deconstructing the Yes/No factor so that the subjects act freely in front of the audience. The subjects become fearless performers that are completely focused on the hypnotist and his/her commands and great show results.

## Myths

There are numerous myths about hypnosis. Here are some frequently asked questions about the myths of hypnotism.
a)_**Can a person stay in a hypnotic state and not wake from it?**
Everyone wakes up out of hypnosis. A person who is hypnotized CANNOT stay in a hypnotic state unless they are constantly hearing the hypnotist's voice. This is the most frequently asked question from audience members after a show. Some people have a true fear in hypnosis that a person can stay in the hypnotic state and not wake up from it. Sometimes a person can be deep enough that they might require a slight tap on the shoulder or an extra count up from the hypnotist, but everyone wakes up from hypnosis. It is very similar to asking, has anyone ever not woken up from a nap? Just as everyone wakes up from a nap, everyone wakes up from a hypnotized state.

## b) Can a person do something that they would not usually do during hypnosis?

This is actually a tricky question for a number of reasons. What someone says they will do and what someone will actually do are different. Amazingly, after hypnosis shows, I have had numerous people come up and say their shy friend would have never acted this way. Their friend could be truly acting out of character on stage. He or she can assume outgoing roles while hypnotized, yet this person could be extremely shy. This question confronts ethical concerns that go beyond the scope of this book, as well of a more detailed understanding of formal education in psychology and hypnosis.

There is an ethical code on stage to keep hypnotized subjects safe at all times. The hypnotist should not give for instance, a suggestion for the subject to experience a plane crash. This suggestion could be given on stage, but is not based on the ethical code. Instead of such careless suggestions, more positive suggestions are given to maintain a safe environment.

The hypnotic subject will naturally protect himself from physical harm under hypnosis. During a stage show, a hypnotist cannot command the person to walk off a five foot high stage and fall onto the ground. The command could be given, but the person would stop before walking off the stage. The hypnotist will create an elaborate story to push the subjects boundaries while always keeping them safe.

An excellent suggestion on stage to push the boundaries is as follows: On the count of three, act as if you are James Bond and walk up to every person you see and say, "My name is Bond, James Bond." This suggestion illustrates how far outside the box hypnotism can lead its subjects. They are literally acting as if they are another character or as if they are an actor on stage, yet they are just in a deep state of hypnosis.

=

## c) Can a person who has been hypnotized remember it afterwards?

There are as many variations of remembering the hypnotic experience as there are personalities being hypnotized. Most people have some recollection of the experience similar to slightly remembering a movie. Some people on stage simply remember nothing at all except for the beginning of the induction, which is the part where the beginning of the hypnosis occurs. This may be due to the fact that a stage hypnotist will say the following before the end of a show: "Any words or suggestions I have made this evening are completely gone from your memory." The hypnotist says this because they do not want some of the suggestions to continue, which does illustrate the power of hypnosis. The suggestion such as a hot/cold skit is an example of this where a hypnotist can influence a subject to feel hot or cold. The suggestions can continue, so the hypnotist does not want them to be present after the show; therefore, the hypnotist removes the suggestion so the subject is always safe and comfortable. As a result, the other skits are forgotten.

d) **Is it really possible to hypnotize people or are they just faking the experience?**

Hypnosis is not the result of a "faked" experience. It is amazing how many people will say, "I don't believe in hypnosis." These comments can come from educated people with strong confidence of disbelief. The best illustration of hypnosis and of how real it is on stage is when someone is hypnotized so that they can go through an entire hypnosis show and not laugh. The entire audience is bursting out in laughter throughout the show, but the hypnotized subjects on stage are not responding to the laughter. The hypnotized subjects on stage are acting as if they have a professional ability to keep a straight face. They are staying within the show by focusing on the hypnotist's voice, and commands. This is evidence of the focused state created by hypnosis. The audience will burst into laughter time and time again since shows can be hilarious, but the subjects will be stone faced as if not even hearing or seeing the humorous scenarios and situations.

The fact that hypnosis exists is undeniable. There are numerous experts that don't believe in hypnosis. However, the reality is there have been numerous studies with EEG (Electroencephalogram) readings that show brain waves are altered under hypnosis. Keep in mind these are the same readings that show sleep is an altered, naturally occurring state.

# CHAPTER 2
# POWER OF SUGGESTION

The power of suggestion is illustrated in numerous areas of our lives. An excellent illustration of this is what is known as the arm levitation technique. Now look at your hands and place both of them out in front of you, palms down. Yes, place both arms out in front of you while you are reading this book. Now, flip your right hand over. Now imagine there is a large set of books in your right hand. As you feel the large set of books in your right hand, imagine your left hand becoming very light. You feel the lightness of your left hand as if there is a balloon in your left hand pulling it up to the ceiling. As you feel your left hand get lighter and lighter, you imagine it pulling up to the ceiling. Now feel the heaviness of the right hand pulling down towards the ground as another set of books is being placed on your right hand. Feel how heavy the right hand is becoming even heavier. Now, Freeze your hands. Look at where your hands are:

This is an illustration of the power of suggestion. The hypnotist gives the commands and describes the story, and your body follows the command or suggestions. You feel as if there is a large set of books in your right hand even though your right hand is completely empty. You feel as if there is a balloon attached to your left arm, but your left arm is completely free. Nothing is attached to your arm, yet your mind creates the images and your body responds. If a hypnotist gives these suggestions to a group of people, a good percentage of the audience will have their hands two or three feet apart when finished like in the illustration to your right. Their left arms will be all the way up and their right arms will be practically to the floor.

## Repetition

When a suggestion is repeated frequently the belief eventually becomes a conviction. An effective hypnotist will use suggestions numerous times in order to create a more solid induction. During a hypnosis show, a stage hypnotist will use the word relax throughout the induction as many as 60 or 70 times. The hypnotist will also use other synonyms to continue the suggestions effectively.

Here is an illustration of this repetition: "The deeper you breathe, the more relaxed you become, the more relaxed you become, the deeper you breathe." One sentence actually has six references to relaxation. The one sentence says "relax," "deeper" and "relaxed," each used twice.

Here is a another example: " Allow your body to drift down deeper within the chair as you feel your body relaxing down. Words like "drift" and "down" are excellent synonyms for "relax." These words get a person into a deeper state of hypnosis.

A third example is as follows: "As you allow your body to relax, you feel your muscles relax." Weaving the suggestions together with repetition allows the subject to get into an even deeper state of hypnosis in a shorter amount of time. Repetition is a key to successful hypnotic sessions both on stage and in an individual session. As said earlier, repetition is a true key to successful hypnotic sessions both on stage and in an individual hypnosis session.

## Stories

What stories have you told yourself throughout life? Think back to your childhood. What stories about life have you heard from friends, family and influential people around you at the time? What are the phrases about money and your ability that you were told? What were the beliefs and stories that you heard from your friends? What was the reality you created from hearing all of these stories? Who told you the stories? What have you retained from these stories? Do you believe you have limited yourself by believing some of these stories? Do you believe these stories have empowered you? On the positive side, what stories have motivated you?

Roger Banister had the belief that he could break the four minute-mile. All of the great experts of the day said that the four minute-mile couldn't be broken. It took Roger Banister's original belief in his own ability in order for him to train and prepare to attempt it.

He achieved this feat on 6 May 1954 at Iffley Road track in Oxford, with Chris Chataway and Chris Brasher providing the pacing. When the announcer declared *"The time was three..."*, the cheers of the crowd drowned out Bannister's exact time, which was 3 min 59.4 sec. (WIkipedia)

One person's belief helped others achieve the four minute mile. Now, thousands of people have achieved the four minute-mile.

## What is Real?

What is real? Imagine yourself grabbing a big, juicy lemon out of the refrigerator. As you grab a knife, slowly slice open the lemon and see the tart lemon juice squirt out of it. Now grab the lemon and taste the citrus, tart in your mouth. While reading this paragraph, is your mouth salivating? Many of us experience this sensation. Your mind accepted the suggestion to envision a lemon and your body reacted to the event as if the lemon was in your mouth. In this situation you experienced hypnosis. The body does not always differentiate what is real and what is imagined. The mind experiences the event as if it happened. You taste the imagined lemon AS IF you had just experienced the taste of the real lemon.

When a person is in a deep enough hypnotic state, he or she can experience even more extraordinary reactions to the suggestions. As a stage hypnotist, I can ask a smaller audience of 50 to 80 people the following: "What do you think of the smell within this bottle? I can open up a bottle that contains only water and give the suggestion, "Do you like the smell of this powerful pine experience?" Many people will raise their hands. They believe they just experienced the smell of a pine forest even though they only experienced water. A person needs minimal hypnosis to experience an imagined sense of smell. The power of suggestions is truly amazing!

--What pictures are you giving yourself that you describe as being real?
--What else in your life are you imagining into reality?
--In what area of your life are you creating the sensation, yet not feeling or acting as if it were true?

If you fall off a building, then you will hit the ground. That is real! Yet, you can also create that same terrifying feeling in a dream or up on stage while hypnotized. Part of the job of a hypnotist on stage during the hypnosis shows is keeping people safe, thus one does not perform a skit similar to this. With on-stage subjects having a feeling like falling a long distance to the ground or any other extremely terrifying experience would be possible, but not ethically responsible. A hypnotist on stage can create a controlled event that instills fear, but it is never wise to create a paranoid or traumatic feeling. The power of hypnosis is so strong that you could, but wouldn't give the following suggestion: "Imagine that you just stepped on a bee-hive." The subjects on stage would go into a frenzy and stand up and run from the bees, while swatting them all around their body. The hypnotist could create a very dangerous situation of potential injury for the subjects. The power of the mind takes over and creates these induced situations. For this reason, the hypnotist does not give such an outrageous suggestion on stage.

A hypnotist on stage can give the following suggestion: "On the count of three, you will imagine yourself on a roller coaster." After the suggestion is given, the subjects will raise their hands and feel as if they are going down the long roller coaster. The subjects could feel their raised heart rate and truly feel the adrenaline rushing through their body. Some of the subjects will even scream out as if they are flying down the roller coaster. This would be a better situation to create on stage since it is a much more controlled suggestion that keeps the subjects within their seats.

These examples show that within certain hypnotic settings, the body does not know the difference between what is real and what is imagined. Imaginary fear in these settings illustrates how hypnosis can create vivid mental imagery of fear inducing scenarios.

Video games are an incredibly powerful illustration of the use of hypnosis and a focused state. The hypnotist will often tell the group at the beginning of a show, "video games are one of the most hypnotic activities you can do in present day life. While playing the game, you feel as if you are actually partaking in what is going on within the screen."

## Person's Expectation

If a person believes that he or she can be hypnotized, then he or she will more readily enter into a state of hypnosis. Many people often ask if you can force someone to do something that they would not ordinarily do while hypnotized. The simple answer is actually yes and no. The trick is this; what someone tells you they will do and what someone will actually do are two totally different things. Hypnosis lowers your inhibitions. Hypnosis breaks down the critical factor: Thus, when someone is told to do something by the hypnotist, he or she just does it. The person does not first say to himself, "Ah, should I do this?" The person simply goes along with the hypnotist in most cases. The hypnotic subject basically cooperates with the commands of the hypnotist without making the conscious decision whether it is a good idea or not.

If a hypnotic subject is asked to describe the experience of being hypnotized, he or she might say: "It feels as if I was just going along with the hypnotist. Was I hypnotized?" Numerous subjects will feel as if they are going along with the event. They will wake up and then realize that an hour has gone by which seems like just 5 minutes. The subjects will often need to verification of time or a video from one of their friends in the audience to believe that they were hypnotized.

# CHAPTER 3
# HYPNOSIS AND THE MEDIA

## Present Day Hypnosis in the Media

We are living in an age where hypnosis has never been so prevalent. In the United States, almost every single person has access to a TV. According to the A.C. Nielsen Co., the average American watches over 4 hours of TV every single day. While watching T.V., a person enters into a hypnotic state. Imagine a person perfectly relaxed on a sofa while he or she is fixated on a point directly in front. The person watching TV is already in a reclined position very similar to a reclined position in a hypnotist's office. The screen is then moving and flashing to create the hypnotic-like focused state. Television is truly the ultimate hypnotic medium and advertisers have figured this out by the simple use of commercials. While you are in this relaxed position being hypnotized by the television show, you are then fed powerful suggestions during the commercial breaks. This happens to us all the time.

Someone can be sitting on their couch watching TV, and his or her spouse can yell from the other room, but the person watching can be so focused he or she simply does not hear the spouse. While in this trance like state watching TV, commercials are inserted within the show as hypnotic suggestions. Advertisers have a clear understanding of the power of the hypnotic trance while watching television. A clear illustration of this is in the

Super Bowl where the average 60 second commercial costs millions of dollars.

The best illustration of the power of hypnosis when it comes to commercials is to look at what is called a post-hypnotic suggestion. While a person is hypnotized on stage, the hypnotist can give the suggestion to have the subject perform a post hypnotic suggestion after they wake from hypnosis. The subject will return to their group of friends in the audience. As a stage hypnotist, I can say to a group while still hypnotized, "Anytime I, and only I, say the word Tarzan, then you will stand up and yell Tarzan at the top of your lungs." When the hypnotized person returns to the audience, anytime the hypnotist then says the word Tarzan, he or she will stand up and yell "Tarzan." The person yells Tarzan immediately. The person that was hypnotized will then sit down and wonder what exactly just happened? The subject will hear the hypnotist and instantly stand up and yell Tarzan at the top of their lungs. What is truly amazing is how instantaneously the subject will stand up and yell. The person does not think to themselves, should I say this or not? The person, simply yells. Now apply this to a commercial and you can see its powerful! Have you ever gone out and bought something and had no clue why you bought it? What are the famous commercials that you personally remember from your childhood and throughout the years? These commercials have been programmed into the public in a similar way to how hypnotist programs the hypnotic suggestion on stage. Considering this power, it is not surprising why the United States has banned the use of cigarette advertising on television. Remember the power of a post hypnotic suggestion.

## The News and Media

In today's world of 24-hour news broadcasting, we encounter many hypnotic suggestions on the news. Sit down on your couch one day and you can turn on the news at any point. Now that they have you in a suggestible state, comfy on your couch, zoned out, they can give you powerful suggestions in order to sway your beliefs one way or another according to their desire. The news station will stream news down below the screen while the commentator is giving the normal news. Frequently, some of the news streaming will be stated as a command which can sway your belief.

Through hypnotic techniques you can see how easily a news station can effect an audience's beliefs. The news never used to be produced like this. On today's 24 hour news channels, your subconscious is being fed the headlines and sub-lines in an incredibly suggestible manner. You are being hypnotized with the news. There are multiple headlines and sub-lines including BREAKING NEWS every other hour. In effect, you are reading the sub headlines but it seems as if they aren't there. They are almost ACTING AS IF they are subliminal messages, even though they are right before your eyes. Streaming these suggestions has become a very rewarding endeavor for the news programs and also very lucrative since they have helped build hypnotized audiences.

## Convince Someone of Anything: Fashion

Fashion perfectly illustrates the suggestible nature of most people. If you sit on a busy street corner in Manhattan, you will potentially see every known form of clothing. The powerful television commercials in the media can convince someone that a pair of pants is worth $300.00 Men and women are convinced every day to wear the most uncomfortable shoes imaginable, as long as they are in fashion.

Sometimes when someone looks back at a yearbook from high school, he or she might be flabbergasted by the fashion that he or she was wearing, but at the time, it looked great. Commercials and the media conveys the idea that a horse can make the price of a simple polo shirt worth more than a normal cotton t-shirt . A good number of these $65.00 shirts can be purchased in a country like Vietnam or Cambodia for the price of $2.00 or $3.00 a shirt. We can end up placing all of this value on fashion through that feeling of 'We Gotta Have It.' The great advertising and numerous hypnotic suggestions add value to the shirt.

One of the most effective and funniest uses of public hypnosis is with expensive travel bags. As a public speaker, traveling through airports, I sometimes see men or women carrying a travel bag by one the high end designers. Many of these bags may cost $400 to $600 dollars. Here is the hilarious catch: They do not have wheels on them. You see the person trudging along carrying this heavy bag sometimes weighing 45 or 50 pounds, and it doesn't even have wheels on it. Truly seasoned travelers carry the bag that has wheels and probably costs a fraction of the price. This is a great illustration that you can convince someone of anything. You can convince someone that the luggage is really worth this exorbitant amount of money.

## Questions to ask yourself:

~~Have we ever been hypnotized by the media?
~~Do we believe that a diamond really buys happiness?
~~Have you ever paid $300 for a pair of jeans?
~~How about the $65.00 rough cotton Polo T shirt. Is it really worth $65.00, or have you been convinced or hypnotized into believing that it is worth $65.00? Is the fact that there is a tiny horse on the shirt that makes it worth so much? How much better is it than the shirt that is one-third the price and made from higher quality of cotton?

This is the real question. Is the media hypnotizing you? Why is it hypnotizing you? The smarter the salesperson and the better the technique, the more effective the sale. Is anyone within the media taking advantage of the public?

# CHAPTER 4
# HYPNOTIZED EASILY

## Easily Hypnotized

One could always ask who is most easily hypnotized? More than anything, a person who is a willing subject will more easily go under than a person who is tense and has passive views towards hypnosis. If you want to be hypnotized or have a willing desire to be hypnotized on stage, then you will be more easily hypnotized. High school and college age people are normally much more open to hypnosis than someone in their mid fifties. This is especially true for a corporate show where people can be very guarded about their behavior. If you would ask any practicing stage hypnotist, if they would rather do a show for a group of high school students in a big theatre or a group of retired people in a big theatre, the answer will always be the high school students. Some of the idea is the great desire to try something new, and sometimes with age people are less likely to try new experiences. This is obviously a generalization and will not always be true.

If a stage hypnotist does a show for 300 high school students then he will normally have more than half of the audience wanting to get on the stage. Sometimes the chairs can't be filled on stage with hypnotist volunteers with an audience in their fifties. Many hypnotists perform for corporate groups of 200 people. When one asks the audience for volunteers, many are often very guarded to get up on stage. Some of this also has to do with the fact that the corporate group is afraid to step outside the box in a corporate setting in front of their peers. One of the real goals of the hypnosis show is to raise the awareness of the world of hypnosis.

## Questions to Ask Yourself:

~~At what point in life do we stop taking chances or trying new activities?

~~At what age do we start truly worrying about what others think so much?

~~At what age do we stop believing in the unknown or doubting the known?

## Time

While under a state of hypnosis, there is a different perception of time. Time can often feel as if it has been eliminated under hypnosis. Hypnosis stage shows last about 60 to 70 minutes and the subjects on stage are normally under hypnosis for about 50 minutes. Before the end of the show, if you ask a person who has been hypnotized on stage, "How long have you been up here? How much time has gone by?" Their answer is mostly two minutes. The hypnotic subject will often say, " I just got up here." The person will think that they just got up on stage. The hypnotist will even ask a question, are you ready to get the show started? Their response will be, "Yes, let's start the show." Even though the subjects have been on stage for 50 minutes, they feel as if it is only a couple of minutes. Once the subjects are told by the hypnotist that it has been almost an hour, there is a look of amazement on their faces. The hypnotized subjects believe they had just gotten on stage. A deep hypnotic state achieved during a hypnosis show is very similar to the time that goes by while we nap or sleep.

## The word Sleep:

Once a person is in a hypnotic state he or she can move around and act out scenarios on stage based on the commands of the hypnotist. If the person slightly comes out the of the state of hypnosis, the hypnotist can look directly into the subject's eyes and say the following command: "SLEEP!" The subject will instantaneously drop down into a sleep like state. The person will instantaneously slump down into the chair as if he or she suddenly fell asleep and his or her body will be back in a deep state of a hypnotic sleep. The power of the word sleep in hypnosis is unbelievable. The audience will always react with a big gasp of amazement as the subject instantly drops down into a sleep like state. This strategy can be used in any hypnotic setting, even therapy. Every repetition of the word sleep increases the subjects' hypnosis depth.

# CHAPTER 5
# THE MOTIVATIONAL

## Use of Vocabulary

WORDS. The study of hypnosis and suggestion is really the study of words. The use of our own vocabulary can be the most powerful thing that we do with ourselves in order to create the life we desire. One of the most important things that a hypnotist must do is to study the careful use of words. During a stage hypnosis event, the hypnotist can tell a hypnotized subject that the chair sitting in front of him or her weighs 500 pounds, and it is impossible to lift. The hypnotized subject looks at the chair and then bends down to lift the chair with all their might, but he or she finds that it is impossible to do so. The hypnotized subject on stage will grimace and try very hard to lift the chair while practically breaking out into a sweat, but they are unable to lift the chair simply because of the hypnotized command. The audience will stare with amazement truly surprised by the hypnotized subjects inability. The hypnotists use of the word "try" controls the subject. Hypnosis is a truly focused state. When suggestions are given to the hypnotized people, the attention of the subjects is on the hypnotist's voice. The subject is not paying attention to the audience or noticing the fan in the background. The subject is simply focused on the suggestions and the wording of the hypnotist. The mind's power is evident. The focus is on the suggestion of the word "try" and the command around "trying" to lift the chair.

As fast as the command was given in hypnosis, it can also be changed or taken away. The hypnotist can give the positive command of "lift the chair," and the subject will successfully lift the chair. Hypnosis truly comes down to commanding the use of words. As a sculptor studies the stone, the hypnotist studies the use of words. The order, the phrasing, and the manner or tone that we use are all major factors in the deepening and maintaining a hypnotic state.

The tone of the hypnotist's voice can also have an a positive or negative effect upon the subject. The deeper, more soothing voice normally hypnotizes a subject better than a squeaky, higher pitched voice. Hypnotists are taught to use the deeper register of their voice, while giving the hypnotic induction. This works much easier if you naturally have a very deep voice. The practice of hypnosis is creating a very deep, monotone pattern to the voice. The voice must also have a commanding presence that instills confidence. The more confident the hypnotist is in his or her ability, the more easily the subject will slip into hypnosis.

In order for the hypnotist's suggestions to be effective, they must be stated in the positive. What does one focus on if you are given the command, " Don't run!" You focus on running! Your mind thus perceives running if you say, "Don't run." It would be better to simply state, " Walk Slowly!" Direct commands are always more effective in hypnosis. Here are some examples of positive commands:
--Relax deeply,
--Allow your body to relax
--Breathe Deeply
--Focus on my voice and only the sound of my voice.
--Feel as if you are a rubber band, and relax
--Allow yourself to sink down in the chair.

Remember to use positive commands in your everyday life as well. In day to day life, the suggestions or commands are always much more effective when stated in the positive.

The simpler the suggestion or command, the more readily someone will respond. A great hypnotist will always tells a wonderful story, but then weaves into the elaborate story commands that are simple and direct! The following is an excellent example: "On the count of three, allow your body to relax. Feel yourself drifting down into the deep, relaxed lounge chair." The command is "drift down in the chair," yet a long, descriptive sentence wraps around the simple command.

Another example would be: "As you feel the muscles of the back on your neck relax, you breathe deeply." The command is "breathe deeply," yet you can keep telling the induction story as you give the command. The words we use have incredibly powerful effective outcomes. If we use the word "try," we will have a more difficult time completing the task than if we used a simple positive command. The better command would be a positive statement of, " I shall lift the chair" or "Lift the chair."

## The Challenge to you:

Use more positive words with your day-to-day life and create your reality!!

Think and be aware of the vocabulary that you use in order to trick or not trick your body into creating situations. If you try to get your work done then you will be much less effective than if you give yourself the command "I will get the work done," or "I am actively getting my work done." If you tell yourself on a day-to-day basis that you are unable to do something then that is the reality that you are creating on a day-to-day basis. If we paint the picture within our suggestion that we might be able to accomplish something, THEN we will create the lifestyle of accomplishing something.

~Create certainty within your life by using words that motivate your body to respond.

~Eliminate the word "Try" from your vocabulary completely.

## Stage Illustrations:

During a stage hypnosis event, the hypnotist can tell certain hypnotized members the following command:
"YOU CAN HEAR MY VOICE, BUT YOU CANNOT SEE ME."
He will then repeat the command to increase its effectiveness.
"YOU CAN HEAR MY VOICE, BUT YOU CANNOT SEE ME."
The hypnotist can then pick up a chair and move the chair back and forth. The chair that was sitting directly in front of the hypnotized subjects is now moving back and forth. The few hypnotized members that the hypnotist chose will be amazed seeing the chair move. The hypnotized subjects will rub their eyes to make sure they are seeing the chair correctly, while they show genuine fear and disbelief! The hypnotized subjects think that the chair is moving by itself. The subjects do not see the hypnotist whatsoever. What is the answer to their amazing reaction? Is it the

fact that they see the hypnotist, but tell themselves that they can't? What would be another potential explanation for this? Is the reality of the subject being changed simply through the suggestions of the hypnotist?

The hypnotist will often have to say to the hypnotized subjects during the the the command, " your butt is glued to the chair and the chair is glued to the ground." The hypnotist makes this statement so that the hypnotized people do not run from the auditorium in a state of genuine fear in their reaction to the chair moving back and forth. The hypnotist will also choose subjects that he or she thinks are unlikely to experience a panic attack or overreact to the suggestion.

Why are the subjects unable to see the chair? The correct term for this is a negative hallucination. A negative hallucination can induce fear like in a movie or real life. Hypnosis can create genuine fear on stage, this tactic is also used in movies.

~What other negative hallucinations are you creating?

~What scenarios in your life are like being unable to see the chair?

Another excellent stage illustration uses the number 7. A hypnotist can say the following command: "On the count of 3, you will forget the number 7. The number 7 is gone from your memory." The hypnotist will then ask the hypnotized person to count from 1 to 10 and they will skip over the number 7. The hypnotist can ask them to count their fingers out loud to the audience and they will once again skip over the number 7 and count 11 fingers. The audience will stand utterly silent amazed by the event. The power of the mind is incredible. This illustration happens in real life when we are trying to introduce a friend to someone else, and we forget their name. You know the person's name, but it is difficult to remember it at that given time. You are saying to yourself, " I know this person's name, but I just simply can't remember it."

Next, it is possible to have someone forget their own name, similar to how you can forget someone else's name. The hypnotist will command, " On the count of three, your name is gone from your memory." The hypnotist will then ask their name and they will simply not be able to remember their name as they are trying with all their might. The subject will have a perplexed look, being unable to remember their own name. The audience of 500 people will be completely silent, amazed that the person is unable to remember their name. You can then ask the following command, " On the count of five, you will remember your name and remember your name as if you are a little kid. Acting as a little kid, you will respond with great excitement as if you are a little kid." The subject on stage will then blurt out their name with a kids voice while showing complete excitement on their entire face. As you can see, hypnosis is used with numerous effective commands on stage.

## Hypnosis and Sport—Golf

Golf. There is probably no single sport that depends more on the mind. Imagine a golfer being at the tee with his pin striped shirt ready to tee off. He has his driver out and takes a couple of practice swings. What is the golfer saying to himself before teeing off? What suggestions is he giving himself for his mind/body to respond to? What ability is he characterizing himself to have?
When teeing off, does the golfer say, " I always hit the fairway," or does the golfer say" I never hit the fairway." Does the player give himself a positive command or a negative command?
There are numerous examples of how hypnosis can and is used within sports. When a golfer is hitting an approach shot towards the green, hypnotic self talk can be used to create a better shot. How many times does a person say before hitting the shot, "I always put it in the trap?" The golfer is focusing on the trap, thus his next shot will be in the trap for his focus was on the trap.
His focus and self talk to himself was not as follows: "On this next shot, I am going to put it on the green." If your self-talk is creating the adventure of being in the sand, then you will simply end up in the sand. The hypnotic self talk should be based on where the golfer would like to hit the ball and not based on what the golfer would like to avoid. The focus becomes the positive verbal commands and not where someone should avoid.

Another excellent example of using hypnosis is before the event begins. What does the golfer tell himself on the way to the course about the next couple of hours on the course? Imagine visualizing the entire round on the way to the course. Create the course within your mind from the deep green, bent grass to the swaying trees. Create the shots within your mind, and create the theatre of the mind when visualizing. See the best round of your life within your golf future. If you believe it to be true, then you go into the simple actions with your body of it being the truth. What is your reaction to a bad shot? What is your perception of the entire round?

The best illustration of someone using hypnotic techniques is the present day pro golfer, Jason Day. He stands before the shot and closes his eyes to visualize it. He will close his eyes and envision the entire shot before he swings. You can see his lips moving at times giving himself positive suggestions in his pre shot routine.

We create suggestions in our mind about the next shot in golf. We create the law of averages when it comes to playing the game. You have heard the saying, "get into the zone." Hypnosis creates the zone. You are in the zone when using hypnosis. Use hypnosis on a more consistent basis to get into the zone that all athletes desire.

# CHAPTER 6
# SLEEP AND RELAX

## Sleep

In order to put one into a state of hypnosis, a hypnotic induction is used. A typical induction lasts about eight to ten minutes. There are numerous induction styles that a hypnotist can use. Each hypnotist will tailor an induction to their style or for the individual they are hypnotizing. The most common form of induction is a technique that uses gradual relaxation. The hypnotist will first get someone into a comfortable position and then get him or her to relax down within the chair. Next, the hypnotist will have them place their hands on their lap and feet on the ground. After that, the hypnotist will say:

"Relax, begin to relax. Focus on your breathing and allow your body to relax. Begin to focus on the muscles in your neck and allow all the muscles in your neck to relax. Next, focus on all the muscles along your back and allow your muscles in your back to drift down. Allowing your body to relax, you feel your body drifting down deeper and deeper. Allow all the muscles in your shoulders to drift down as you feel your body drifting down as your enter into a state of relaxation. As you feel your arms relax, you allow your body to relax as you feel yourself relaxing down deeper and deeper. The deeper you breathe, the more relaxed you become, the more relaxed you become the deeper you breathe. Now feel the relaxation moving into your arms and drifting down your arms into your hands. Feel yourself relaxing down as you allow your hands to relax. You feel your body sinking down deeper and deeper within the chair. Now allow the relaxation to move into the lower and deeper part of your back as you allow yourself to relax. Now as you act as if your legs are relaxing down deeper and deeper. Feel the muscles in your thighs relax as the relaxation drifts down into the lower, deeper part of your legs, now allow this relaxation to move slowly into your feet as you allow your feet to relax."

"The deeper you breathe, the more relaxed you become, the more relaxed you become, the deeper you breathe."

This illustration is one of the hypnotic inductions that can be used on stage. Notice the number of times, the word relax is used within the paragraph. Now, imagine practicing this technique yourself while you are going to sleep. Many of us, have a difficult time while falling asleep as our thoughts race through our minds. We toss and turn or take a sleep aid in a version of a pill in order to allow one to sleep. A better solution of the sleep problem could be to use a gradual relaxation technique. One can use a gradual relaxation technique by using guided relaxation similar to hypnosis in a sleep CD or a sleep app which would induce sleep using gradual relaxation techniques.

Realize the power of suggestion when you lie down at night to relax. You feel your body drifting down into a deep and relaxed state. These suggestions can be used be to help you fall asleep. A sleep CD or app can help you sleep by using the natural way or the power of your mind. As we learn to use gradual relaxation better, we can better fall asleep when we find ourselves tossing and turning. There are numerous methods that a hypnotist can us for gradual relaxation, and the first one that we will explore is the counting down effect.

MESMER'S TUB;

# INDUCTION TECHNIQUES

## Counting Down

The next part of the induction is what a hypnotist refers to as the counting down technique. Any numbers can be used within the counting down technique, and for this illustration we will countdown from 10 to 1. WALKING DOWN A LONG STAIRCASE.
Imagine yourself focusing on a long staircase. As you see the long staircase before you, you see yourself walking down the long staircase. As you feel your body walking down the long staircase, you feel as if your body is drifting down. As you feel your body drifting down, we count backwards from 10 to 1. Allow your body to drift down as we count backwards from 10 to 1. Drifting down

deeper and deeper. Notice the deeper you breathe, the more relaxed you become and the more relaxed you become, the deeper you breathe. Feel your body drifting down the long staircase. As we count backwards from 10 to 1, you feel your body relaxing down. 10, 9. Allowing your body to drift down the long staircase, 8, 7, feeling your body drifting down the long staircase, 6, 5. 4 even deeper as you allow your body to relax down, 3, 2 . Allowing your body to drift down even deeper down the long staircase. The deeper you breathe, the more relaxed you become, the more relaxed you become, the deeper you breathe.

## The Lounge Chair

Now imagine yourself sinking down into a deep and relaxed lounge chair. Feel yourself drifting down into the relaxed lounge chair as all of your limbs begin to feel like loose, limp rubber bands. Now, imagine yourself sinking down into a deep and relaxed lounge chair on the beach and looking up at the big white, puffy clouds. As you look up at the big, white puffy clouds, you will notice that they will form numbers. 10, 9. Drifting down deeper within the lounge chair. As you feel yourself relaxing down in the lounge chair, you allow your body to relax. 8, 7. Now, feel your body relaxing down deep within the chair. 6, 5 the numbers drift you down into a more relaxed state. 4, 3. Allowing your body to relax. 2, 1 now you feel yourself ten times more relaxed. You feel your body entering into a very, deep relaxed state. A very, deep and relaxed hypnotic state as you feel your body drifting down into the deep and relaxed lounge chair. Now that your body is in the lounge chair, allow your body to relax down even deeper. This is an excellent example of using the lounge chair and the focus of the induction. One can always visualize the subjects sinking deeply into their chairs while using this induction.

## Hypnosis. The Further Induction.

Now imagine yourself sinking down into a deep, relaxed lounge chair. You feel the big, white puffy pillows in the lounge chair as you allow yourself to drift down deeper and deeper.

Allow your body to continue to relax down, as you feel yourself sinking down deeper into the chair. The deep, relaxed lounge chair drifts your body down as you feel yourself relaxing down.

Allowing your body to relax down allows your body to relax. Remember, very easily, relax and drift down.

Notice once again the repetition of the word relax. As you allow your body to relax, you feel your body relax. While on stage as a hypnotist you want the words to flow. You want your words to flow like a song, not as a choppy, non-rhythmic sentence. Getting the person in a relaxed state is half the battle to getting him or her into a hypnotic state.

Another great use of hypnotic language uses the phrases "picture yourself," "act as if" and "allow yourself." One of the most effective language uses in hypnosis is the words "ACT AS IF". On the count of three, ACT AS IF, you are canoeing along a beautiful river with your paddle in your hand. The person naturally, hypnotically responds and ACTS AS IF he or she is paddling the canoe. They have their hands out in front of them taking long, clean strokes. The second term is the word, PICTURE YOURSELF. Now, picture yourself, paddling along the beautiful river. Now you see off in the distance, there are some people off the island. Picture yourself paddling along, now grab your binoculars and zoom in to the people on the island. As you see the people on the island, you zoom in a bit closer. Imagine the people on the island and zoom in there a bit closer and really get a good look at the people on the island. "Picture yourself," "allow yourself," "ACT AS IF" are all very effective uses of the hypnotic language.

The language you use in hypnosis helps guide a hypnotic subject. Under hypnosis, the hypnotist is the guide just as the movie guides the imagination or the words of the book guide your mental imagery. The better the hypnotist, the more vivid the language used to describe the event or scenario that the hypnotist would like to have the person act out. The hypnotic commands are always very short, clear and concise, but the story that the hypnotist creates for the subject is always dotted with very colorful and vivid language.

## Physical signs a person is hypnotized

What are the physical signs that a person has entered into a hypnotic state? There are 50 different levels to classify a subjects depth of hypnosis. What are the signs that a hypnotist looks for in the subjects on stage or during a hypnotic session to see if they are in a deep state of hypnosis?

With the lighter stages of hypnotic sleep, a person begins to bow their head as he or she relaxes down into the chair. A stage hypnotist can see the subject's eyelids as their eyelids flutter at a rapid rate.

Another sign that the person is becoming deeply hypnotized is the relaxing of the hands. The subject's hands and arms will begin to slump down as if he or she is falling down into the chair. The subject's arms and hands will look as if they are loose, limp rubber bands folding down into the chair. There will be a lightness to the hands as if the subject has fallen asleep within the chair. Often times, the arms will slide off their laps and drape down the subject's sides.

Possibly the best illustration of a person in a deep state of hypnosis is the stillness one exhibits while hypnotized. The hypnotized subject will demonstrate a complete lack of fidgeting The typical hypnotic induction lasts eight to ten minutes and the hypnotized person will continue to drift down deep within the chair. Once the hypnotic subject is in the deep, relaxed state, the subject will not fidget whatsoever. The person is in a completely relaxed state without scratching his or her nose, or moving positions within the chair. Try sitting for two minutes alone without moving whatsoever in a chair. It is incredibly challenging. When not in a hypnotic state, we will fidget within the chair, moving around, and adjusting our bodies, or scratching our bodies.

When a subject on stage is fidgeting, it is the number one sign that the subject is not deep enough to work with on stage. The hypnotist at that point will politely ask the person to return to the audience and watch the rest of the show from there with the rest of the group. Audience members will often be amazed with how still the hypnotic subjects are while under a state of hypnosis. One would have to have a considerable knowledge of hypnosis to fool a seasoned hypnotist into faking that he or she was hypnotized.

## The Word Sleep.

After the hypnotist gets the subjects into a deep, relaxed state of sleep, the hypnotist can give the powerful command of "SLEEP!" The command would sound like this: "Whenever I say the word sleep, your body will drift down into a deep, relaxed state no matter where you are or what you are doing." When this command is said, the hypnotized subject instantly slump down in his or her chair a completely relaxed state as if they fell asleep in the chair. This can be used very effectively on stage. The hypnotic subject can be moving around doing an act that the hypnotist suggested, and then the hypnotist can give the command, SLEEP. The person will instantly sink down deep into the chair. The hypnotized person will look like he or she is completely out of it. His or her head will be slumped over with legs languidly relaxed and arms draped over in the chair. It is as if the subject instantly falls asleep. Just by saying the word, "SLEEP" the person will instantly drop down into a deep, state of hypnosis.

## The Post Hypnotic Suggestion:

While hypnotizing a group on stage, the hypnotist can use what is called a post hypnotic suggestion toward the end of the show. The post hypnotic suggestion is used after the hypnotist wakes the subjects out of a state of hypnosis, and is also used when they return to the audience to sit down with their friends. The post hypnotic is a hypnotic suggestion used for when the subject comes out of a state of hypnosis versus when they are in the state of hypnosis up on stage. The post hypnotic suggestion is basically the future tense of hypnosis. The hypnotist will say the following, " Whenever I, and only I, say the word red, you will stand up and yell the word, Tarzan." The command is incredibly effective as the person will suddenly stand up and yell, "Tarzan."

Surprisingly, the hypnotist can suggest a command that the subject follows in the future. One can give the command, " In 22 minutes, you will stand up and scratch your neck, and the person will automatically stand up and scratch their neck 22 minutes later.. An example of a future hypnosis suggestion could be as follows: "While you return to the audience and I give the command OH YES, you will stand up and yell, "OH YEH!." The person will then stand up when they return to the audience and quietly sit down within the chair. The hypnotist will continue to talk to the audience and discuss the uses of hypnosis and thank people for coming to the show. The hypnotist will then say the word "OH YES, and then the hypnotic subjects that were up on stage will stand up and yell, "OH YEH!" The subjects will then sit back down as if nothing had happened.

The subject's quick reaction to a post hypnotic is incredible! The subject will snap into the command as fast as the hypnotist snaps his fingers. Boom. The hypnotized subject will stand up and DO the command. The subject will stop whatever task he or she is doing in the audience, stand up and shout the command. The power of the mind is truly unbelievable.

The Post Hypnotic suggestions mirror how a commercial works. We are sitting in our living room being hypnotized by the fluttering of the TV screen flashing images of a TV show at us, when suddenly a commercial comes over the air and we are watching it. We are in a hypnotized state already while watching the T.V., and then we receive the commercial. The powerful suggestions of the commercial both visually and vocally are then given to us in this deep hypnotic state. Commercials are really just post hypnotic suggestions. Days or weeks later, we will go out and buy something without even knowing where we initially formed the idea. Suddenly we wonder why we decide to buy the certain toilet paper while we are at the grocery store when we actually have seen the commercial numerous times before without even knowing it.

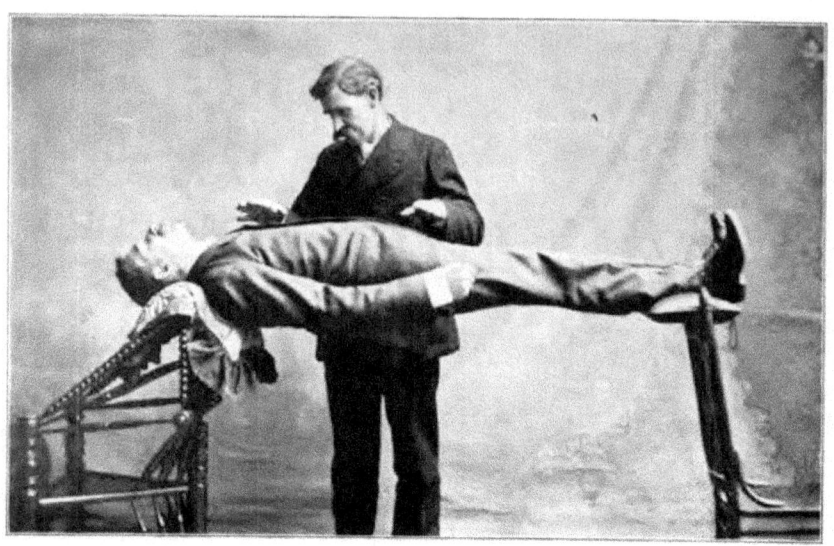

## Hypnosis: Between Two Chairs:

An amazing illustration of the focused state used in hypnosis is what is known as the "stiff as a board chair technique." During a hypnosis show, a hypnotist can take a very suggestible person in a deep, deep state of hypnosis. The subject is then put into the deepest state of hypnosis and told to act as if they are stiff as a board. After the person is acting as stiff as a board, two chairs are placed about five feet apart. The person is then picked up by volunteers and placed with their feet on one chair and their shoulders placed on the other chair. The hypnotized subject will not fall between the two chairs. The illustration above will explain this visually. This is an outstanding example of the power of the mind and the power of hypnotic suggestion. The power of suggestion truly can create limitless possibilities.

# CHAPTER 7

# THE CONCLUSION

What is ultimately possible under hypnosis? What does the future have to hold for hypnosis? What can you do with utilizing the techniques of hypnosis in your everyday life? Will there be continued research on the power of the mind using hypnotic techniques? What hypnotic techniques will be used in the future that will be called something different than hypnosis?

## Conclusion

What reality are you ultimately creating on a day-to-day basis? What stories are you listening to and accepting as fact? What words are you using to influence yourself? Who is hypnotizing you on a day-to-day basis?

Imagine yourself creating your own reality! Allow the words you use to create amazement in your life!! Remember the suggestions that you give yourself help to create the life that you ultimately want. Use hypnosis to your advantage, instead of letting others use hypnosis in order to control you. Create situations that allow you to use hypnosis for your benefit.

## ABOUT THE AUTHOR

Gabriel Holmes is a stage hypnotist/public speaker and has performed over 1300 shows to date all over North America. Gabriel comes from a team building and stage entertainment background. He received his undergraduate degree from Bucknell University in Lewisburg, Pennsylvania and later received his hypnosis training in Boston, Massachusetts. Gabriel lives in Minnesota and has a zest for travel.

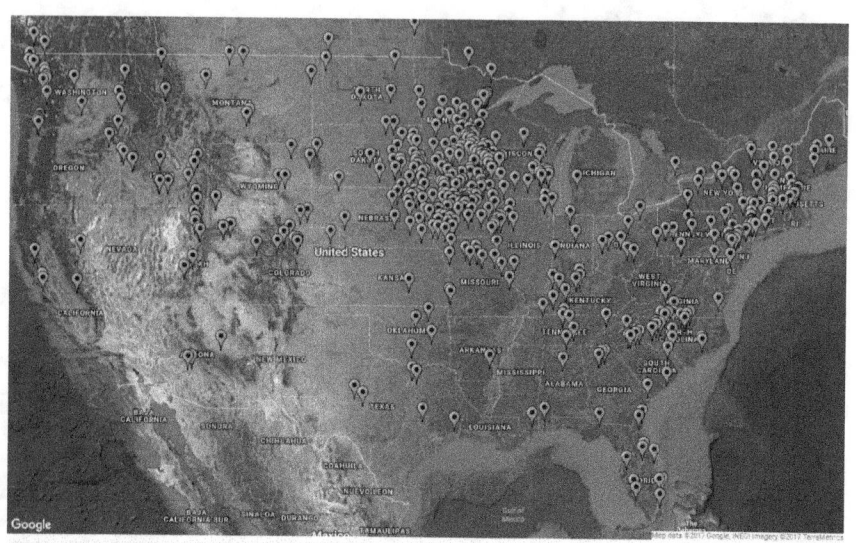

The over 1300 shows thus far.